NEW YORK

NEW YORK

SUZANNE LEVERT

Franklin Watts
New York/London/Toronto/Sydney/1987
A First Book

Cover photographs courtesy of:
New York State Department of Commerce; Shostal;
New York Convention & Visitors Bureau.

Photographs courtesy of:
New York Convention & Visitors Bureau: pp. 11, 35,
36, 39, 41, 42, 46, 47, 49, 50, 53; New York State
Department of Commerce: pp. 12, 57, 59, 63, 64, 66, 68,
70, 73, 74, 77, 80; Library of Congress: p. 20; Canal
Museum, Syracuse, N.Y.: p. 23; Photograph by Byron, The
Byron Collection, Museum of the City of New York: p, 24;
U.S. Army Photo: p. 60; New York Power Authority: p. 79.

Library of Congress Cataloging-in-Publication Data

LeVert, Suzanne.
New York.

(A First book)
Bibliography: p.
Includes index.
Summary: Discusses the history and geography of
New York state and its largest city.
1. New York (State)—Juvenile literature. 2. New
York (N.Y.)—Juvenile literature. [1. New York
(State) 2. New York (N.Y.)] I. Title.
F119.3.L48 1987   974.7   87-6175
ISBN 0-531-10390-0

CONTENTS

NEW YORK

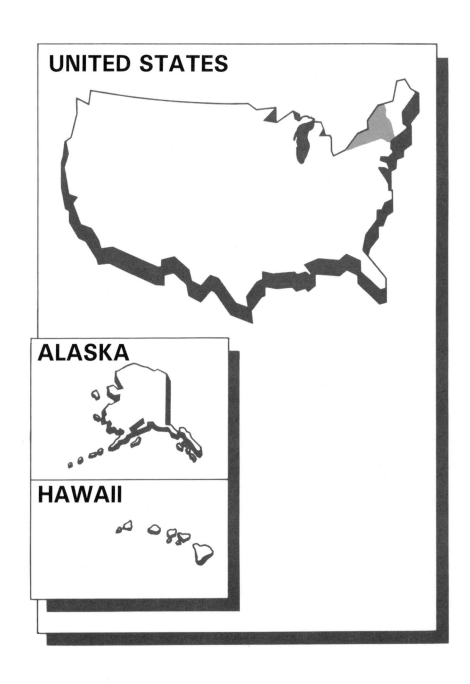

UNITED STATES

ALASKA

HAWAII

1

THE EMPIRE STATE: AN OVERVIEW

The Empire State—how majestic that nickname is. And how right it is to describe New York as a powerful land. Our eleventh state has been on the leading edge of America's progress and growth since the beginning of our history.

To many people, New York means New York City, the most densely populated 301 square miles (780 sq km) in the United States. The "Big Apple," as it is fondly known, is packed with nearly 7.5 million people of every ethnic, racial, and economic background. Over half of all immigrants to the United States have passed through New York Harbor, and many of them settled right in the city. People from all over the world have contributed their cultures and energies to this great city, lending it a very special vitality and excitement.

A towering vista of skyscrapers enhances this excitement. The New York City skyline is one of the most magnificent sights in the world. The Empire State Building, the World Trade Center, and the gleaming white facade and sparkling glass tower of the United Nations building are just a few of the city's architectural wonders.

—9

In banking and finance, publishing and painting, theater and music, fashion and dance, New York City is considered by many to be the most important city in the world. Wall Street, the financial district, houses some of the most powerful institutions of world trade and economy. Hundreds of multinational corporations and banking institutions have their headquarters there.

In the creative arts, too, New York City's influence is overwhelming. Numerous museums, galleries, legitimate theaters, and movie theaters are scattered among the city's many diverse neighborhoods. The high concentration of these showplaces, and the vast numbers of residents who enjoy them, have made New York City the center of the arts in America, perhaps in the world. Almost every major U.S. publishing house is headquartered there, and the fashion industry blossoms along Seventh Avenue.

Artists in every field—theater, music, art—flock to New York City. They come for the excitement of being among other artists, for the stimuli provided by the fast pace and diverse cultural influences, and for the chance to be recognized by the critical audience of sophisticated New Yorkers. As the song made famous by Frank Sinatra puts it, "If I can make it there, I'll make it anywhere!"

THE "OTHER" NEW YORK

Away from the footlights and the skyscrapers, there is another New York. This New York is full of natural wonders—its skyscrapers are snowcapped mountains, its footlights are sparkling lakes, its thrills come from ski jumping, waterskiing, and hiking through forests teeming with wildlife.

Upstate New York lies north and west of the New York City metropolitan area and has its own great traditions. It has some of the most fertile farmland in the country. Second only to California in wine production, second only to Washington state in apple harvest, and one of the leading dairy producers in the country, New York State is indeed quite proud of its agricultural output. Over 50

The Statue of Liberty raises her torch in welcome.
The twin towers of the World Trade Center
dominate Lower Manhattan's skyline. In the
distance at the left is the Empire State Building;
on the far right is the Brooklyn Bridge.

A tranquil scene in upstate New York

percent of the state is covered by trees, and large tracts of wilderness remain undeveloped. The largest state park system in the country provides New Yorkers and visitors with ample opportunities to enjoy this splendor.

Over 90 percent of all New Yorkers live in urban areas, almost half in New York City, and the rest in the six major cities in upstate New York. Albany, Buffalo, Syracuse, Rochester, Utica, and Binghamton have each provided millions of citizens employment in many diverse manufacturing and industrial jobs. The products produced— fine clothing; important metals, minerals, and energy resources; leather and leather products; eyeglasses and scientific instruments—have provided the nation with many of the things it has needed to grow into the wealthy and vital country it is today.

New York is lucky in another respect as well. Many other northeastern states have suffered as the nation's economy has shifted from manufacturing to more service-related jobs, such as finance, real estate, and tourism. But New York has been strong in these service areas all along. Now that it can focus on expanding its economy in this direction, New York State is leading the country in adjusting to this fundamental change.

THE GREAT STATE
OF CONTRASTS

Cold winters, hot summers. High mountain peaks, sandy ocean beaches. Bustling cities, huge expanses of wilderness. Geographically, New York is a rich and varied state.

In other aspects as well, stark contrasts exist. Some of the richest people in the country live in New York, and some of the poorest. The largest state park system coexists with congested, ugly city slums. Families who can trace their American ancestry back to colonial times live near the most recent immigrants from Central America, Korea, and Southeast Asia. Tiny shops owned by industrious individuals struggle to survive while multinational companies compete in the world market.

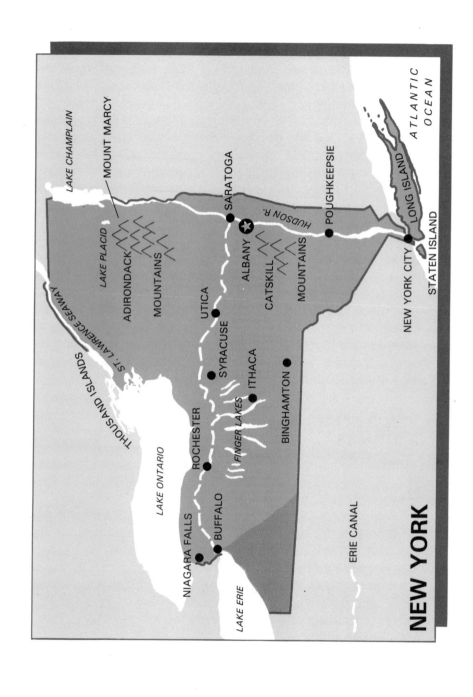

NEW YORK

NIAGARA FALLS
LAKE ERIE
ERIE CANAL
BUFFALO
LAKE ONTARIO
ROCHESTER
FINGER LAKES
THOUSAND ISLANDS
ST. LAWRENCE SEAWAY
SYRACUSE
UTICA
ITHACA
BINGHAMTON
ADIRONDACK
MOUNTAINS
LAKE PLACID
MOUNT MARCY
LAKE CHAMPLAIN
SARATOGA
ALBANY
HUDSON R.
CATSKILL
MOUNTAINS
POUGHKEEPSIE
NEW YORK CITY
STATEN ISLAND
LONG ISLAND
ATLANTIC
OCEAN

One of the most interesting contrasts is that between New York City and New York State. New York City is in many ways big and powerful enough to be a state of its own. And because of its size, density, and ethnic and economic diversity, it has needs and strengths different from the rest of the state. The people who are drawn to a big city like New York tend to want different things from their work and for their personal lives than do small-town or rural dwellers.

The differences between the city and upstate communities can also be illustrated by their political division. Although this trend is changing, most upstate New Yorkers have traditionally voted Republican and have been more conservative in their politics and approach to life. Many New York City dwellers, on the other hand, have tended to be Democrats and supporters of liberal causes.

Despite these many contrasts, and maybe because of them, New York State has remained strong and vital. It has used its resources to create one of the most extensive public transportation systems in any American state. An intricate system of canals links its great rivers and lakes to the Atlantic Ocean. Fine libraries, hospitals, colleges, and universities abound throughout the state.

Without a doubt, however, it is the great people of New York who really set their state apart. The artists, financiers, shopkeepers, craftspeople, tradespeople, farmers, and others all contribute to make the Empire State shine. New York has given the United States seven presidents, nine vice-presidents, and hundreds of great political leaders.

EXCELSIOR
(EVER UPWARD):
A HISTORY

The very first residents of what is now New York State were probably Algonkian Indians. Algonkians are a group of tribes that have separate identities but speak similar dialects and have similar customs. The Algonkian tribes were spread out all over the eastern part of North America and have lived in New York for over 10,000 years.

Along the Hudson River and the shores of many of New York's lakes and rivers, the many different Algonkian tribes, including the Mohican, Lenni Lenape, and Mohawk, had set up small communities. They hunted and fished in New York's plentiful forests and waters and lived in shelters made of bark and woven mats called wigwams. Animal skins, sewn together by the women, provided their clothing. While the Algonkians were not an especially aggressive group of tribes, they were skilled in warfare and ready to fight for their territory.

One of their first enemies was another group of tribes, the Iroquois. While the Algonkians were intelligent, strong, and brave, they were no match for the Iroquois. Not only were the Iroquois clever warriors, they were also very ambitious and politically very sophisticated. One source of Iroquois power was their confederacy. In the mid-sixteenth century, a member of the Huron tribe recognized the need for unity among the various Iroquois tribes. In numbers there is strength, this brave man named Deganawida reasoned, and in strength there is peace. He managed to convince his fellow Iroquois of this wisdom, and the Five Nation Confederacy was formed, made up of the Mohawk, Oneida, Onondaga, Cayuga, and Seneca tribes.

The tribes would need their strength, for in the early 1600s, the European settlers arrived in full force. Settlers would fight these American Indians without mercy for the rich territory that was New York. Thousands of Indians were killed, and the land they had nurtured was taken from them. Treaties were made with those who could no longer fight. As part of these treaties, more land was taken from them. Indians were forced to live on reservations, land the white people didn't want.

Today nearly 40,000 American Indians live in New York State, 12,000 on reserved lands. Many live in poverty. It is a great tragedy of American history that these once strong and cultured people were so destroyed. They are now struggling to regain their identities and assert their rights. Many in New York and elsewhere are fighting to reclaim the land they feel is rightfully theirs.

THE EUROPEANS ARRIVE

The first European ever to gaze upon the shore of what would become New York was Giovanni da Verrazzano, a Florentine in the service of the king of France. Looking for a western passage to the Orient, Verrazzano sailed into New York Harbor in 1524. Impressed by the beauty of what he saw, he reported back to the king: "It seemed so commodious and delightful, and which we supposed must contain great riches."

But it would be another eighty-five years before the first European settlers would arrive. In 1609, Henry Hudson, an Englishman employed by the Dutch, navigated the mighty river that would later be named for him. A few years later, the Dutch flag was planted in a settlement then called Fort Orange, later Albany. In 1626, one of the most profitable real estate deals in history was made on the island of Manhattan. For about twenty-four dollars worth of things the Indians valued, the Dutch governor of the colony, Peter Minuit, bought the entire island from the Indians.

Although the Dutch wanted the colony, called New Netherland, as a trading post, they had no real interest in populating it. Unlike many of the other European settlers, the Dutch were not fleeing any religious or economic troubles at home. When the more aggressive English sailed into New York Harbor in 1663, ready to fight for control of this rich paradise, the Dutch gave it up easily. King Charles II of England made a present of the colony to his brother James, Duke of York, and the colony was renamed the Province of New York after him.

Soon the population of New York was blossoming. Dutch, French, German, and British colonists arrived by the boatload, settling along the shores of the Hudson. Black slaves were imported and did much of the farming in the early colonial days. Although New York would later become a center for the antislavery movement and one of the first states to free its slaves, it played a very real part in the early days of the slave trade.

THE AMERICAN REVOLUTION

On July 9, 1776, the Provincial Congress of New York met at the town of White Plains and ratified the Declaration of Independence. Tired of their finances and political affairs being controlled by the crown back in England, the colonists decided to revolt against their rulers.

This decision was by no means unanimous among the 163,000 citizens then living in New York. In fact, of all the thirteen colonies, it was New York that had the most loyalists. The bloody, painful Revolution must have seemed like a civil war to many New Yorkers, as one neighbor set himself against another.

Nearly one-third of all the battles of the American Revolution were fought on New York soil. The Mohawk Valley, the shores of Long Island, and the settlements around Lake Champlain in the northern part of the state, were the primary battlegrounds. New York City itself was occupied by the British for most of the war.

When General George Washington marched into New York City on November 25, 1783, he signaled the end of the war. He took the oath of office as the nation's first president in New York City on April 30, 1789, and the city served as the capital of the United States from 1785 to 1790.

EXPANSION AND TRANSPORTATION

After the Revolution, a wholehearted effort at expansion northward and westward took place. Clearings were made in the dense wilderness. Log cabins, brick and stone houses, and sawmills were built, and land was cultivated. Villages sprang up. Churches, schools, and town halls were created.

It was during this time that New York's fantastic transportation system began to be formulated. New York was now the largest state in the Union, and it needed an efficient way for goods and people to travel within the state. Turnpikes, linking one large village to another, branched out. While these roadways could be very helpful, they were also very rough and frequently impassable. Although roadways were clearly essential, New Yorkers were neglecting their prime form of transportation—water.

If a water route could be devised that could carry supplies from New York City, on the Atlantic Coast, up the Hudson River and

Many Revolutionary War battles were fought throughout the state. Here a soldier's wife helps out at Fort Niagara.

across to Lake Erie, much time and money could be saved and opportunities for expansion fulfilled. It would take a great person with incredible tenacity to make this vision a reality.

DEWITT CLINTON AND THE ERIE CANAL

The Clinton family—Charles, his two famous sons, James and George, and grandson DeWitt—dominated New York politics during its first fifty years. Charles was a farmer, surveyor, and land speculator and did much to expand New York's territory. James was a judge and a Revolutionary War officer. George, a brilliant politician, served as governor of New York for seven consecutive terms between 1777 and 1801. Later, he served as vice-president under Thomas Jefferson and James Madison. DeWitt held almost every public office in New York, including assemblyman, mayor of New York City, and governor of New York.

The Erie Canal was DeWitt's most lasting accomplishment. He urged the building of this enormous project in order to make "the desert bloom like a rose." He knew that New York's central position in early America made it a perfect, natural gateway from the East to a burgeoning West. And New York City's location on the Atlantic meant that foreign markets were readily accessible, too.

But Clinton had a hard time getting the New York legislature to see this logic. Too many New York City lawmakers saw the Erie Canal as an extremely expensive "upstate" project. This time, though, upstate won. The canal finally stretched an impressive 363 miles (584 km), spanning the state from Albany on the Hudson to Buffalo on Lake Erie. It was completed in 1825.

Since then, the canal system has been enlarged and improved. In 1918, the Barge Canal was completed. This system of fifty-seven locks spanning 845 miles (1,360 km) connects Lake Erie with Lake Champlain, Lake Ontario, and the Cayuga and Seneca lakes. In 1959, the St. Lawrence Seaway opened, connecting the St. Lawrence River with the Great Lakes. Today, ships move millions of tons of goods to and from more than 100 cities along these waterways.

When the age of the railroad began in the mid-1800s, New York was a leader in this area as well. The first New York railroad, which opened in 1831, connected Albany and Schenectady, and, in the years that followed, thousands more miles of track were laid. Today 4,000 miles (6,400 km) of railroad track are in use.

Now, of course, the automobile and airplane dominate transportation in the state as elsewhere. The Thomas E. Dewey State Thruway, a four-lane highway, is part of the 15,000-mile (24,000-km) state highway system. Three hundred sixty-five airports, including John F. Kennedy International, the largest air cargo port in the world, make their home in New York today.

NEW YORK COMES OF AGE

In the middle to late 1800s, an enormous change took place in this country and other parts of the world. New inventions and technology allowed manufacturing and industry to become possible on a large scale, in New York and across America. The economy, which had been based on agriculture and commerce, shifted to these new concerns. Iron was mined, steel was manufactured, and products of all types were mass-produced in huge factories that were built in towns and cities across the country.

Millions of people were needed to work in these factories. A huge shift in population took place as people moved from rural areas into the cities, and nowhere was this more true than in New York. Its resources—waterpower, metals and minerals, and an intricate transportation system—made it the center of industry in the country.

While the Industrial Revolution brought prosperity to the state, this prosperity came at a high human cost. Factories were crowded and unsafe. There were no child labor laws, no minimum wages, no health insurance or workman's compensation.

*View of a boat approaching the
Lockport Locks from the East, about 1825.*

*People from rural parts of the country as well
as immigrants from Europe flocked into
New York's cities during the late 1890s.*

In addition, people were flooding into New York's cities by the hundreds of thousands. Some came from the region's rural areas; most were recently arrived immigrants from the European countries of Poland, Germany, Ireland, and Russia. All were looking for work. This influx of people created many problems—overcrowding in inadequate housing, unsanitary conditions, and a growing underclass of poverty-stricken human beings living amid this filth.

While these conditions could be found in any of the factory towns in New York State, they were most significant in New York City. At the same time that skyscrapers and stately mansions were being built by wealthy industrialists, slum neighborhoods where the workers lived were growing at an alarming rate. By 1900 over 1.5 million people, mostly immigrants, were living in squalid slums.

New York had come of age, and it had to face its problems before it was overtaken by them. Fortunately, the state had a remarkable gift for producing great political leaders—people with vision and integrity who would see New York through its darkest times, find its great strengths, and help it to fulfill its destiny as one of America's leading states. Many great activists and politicians would take the helm in both the capital of Albany and in New York City in the decades that followed.

Alfred E. Smith, who was governor of New York from 1918 to 1926, made dramatic changes in the way the state was run. He pruned the government's overgrown bureaucracy. He revamped the tax system and poured money into public programs for parks, highways, bridges, hospitals, and schools. He instituted labor laws to protect the workers—men, women, and children.

Franklin Delano Roosevelt, who succeeded Smith as governor, continued and expanded these reforms. When the economic collapse of the Great Depression took place in the 1930s, New York was especially hard hit. Roosevelt instituted the country's first coordinated state aid to cities and towns with the Temporary Emergency Relief Administration in 1931. He was elected president of the United States the next year.

Back home in New York, Herbert Lehman, a strong supporter of Roosevelt's policies, became governor. In New York City, a dynamic politician named Fiorello (Little Flower) La Guardia was elected mayor of New York. With the help of these bright and vibrant men, New York survived the Depression. New York City, in fact, experienced somewhat of a building boom during the 1930s. Under the leadership of Parks and Planning Commissioner Robert Moses, new roadways, pools, playgrounds, and parks were built. The Empire State Building, then the tallest building in the world, was completed in 1931. Rockefeller Center, a ten-block area of skyscrapers and outdoor plazas, the hallmark of the city, was built in the eight years that followed.

POST–WORLD WAR II BOOM

When the United States emerged victorious from World War II in 1945, the whole country experienced an economic and population boom. New York was no exception. Upstate, companies such as General Electric, IBM, Bausch & Lomb, Eastman Kodak, and Xerox began to expand and were on their way to becoming the enormous corporations they are today. Governors Dewey, Harriman, and Rockefeller saw that funds were raised for ambitious public projects such as state university and highway systems. The St. Lawrence Seaway, which opened the Great Lakes to ocean shipping, was also completed at this time.

The state's population experienced new growth as another wave of immigration took place shortly after the war. Blacks came from the South in record numbers, and new arrivals from Puerto Rico poured into New York at the rate of 1,000 per week during the 1950s. At the same time, the new highways being built across the state and in New York City made access to the city possible. Now middle- and upper-class workers could move out of the crowded inner city, live in the suburbs, and still commute easily into the city every day. This change in population set the stage for a crushing urban crisis in the 1960s and 1970s.

URBAN CRISIS

The slums and ghettos of New York City were not just products of the sweatshops and factories of the 1800s. As more and more people flocked to the cities to find work, which was no longer plentiful, a permanent underclass of poor, unskilled, and undereducated people was created. They lived in crowded tenement buildings in depressed neighborhoods. When the tax base further eroded as middle- and upper-class people fled to the suburbs, and as the nation's economy began to shift to the Sunbelt in the South and West, city services began to deteriorate. Schools were understaffed and underfunded. Police and sanitation budgets were cut, and ghetto areas suffered most from the lack of protection and services.

Racial tensions also reached a peak in the 1960s as the fight for civil rights brought blacks into the streets. Angry and bloody riots broke out in the slums of New York City and other urban areas in New York as blacks demanded equal opportunity. In a land of plenty, there was an ugly underside of racism and poverty.

In an effort to keep the city from completely falling apart, its leaders, including Governor Nelson Rockefeller, embarked on a massive program to aid neighborhoods, keep the mass-transit system running, and give the poor some desperately needed opportunities. Because the Vietnam War was diverting federal funds that might have helped ease the state's financial burden, the state had to borrow more and more money. When the nation experienced a deep recession in the 1970s, New York City was in desperate shape. The city had lost nearly 600,000 jobs by 1974. Its credit had dried up—it could no longer borrow the money it needed to keep going. In 1975, New York City was over $1 billion in debt and came within moments of declaring bankruptcy.

CITY AND STATE—
I LOVE NEW YORK

But New York City pulled itself together, thanks largely to the Mutual Assistance Corporation, developed by financier Felix Rohatyn and Governor Hugh Carey. This agency was a unique combination of state, city, and private initiatives to refinance the city. Because of this organization's solid financial base, the federal government stepped in with some help of its own. Slowly, the city grew stronger and the relationship between city and state took on a new air of interdependence and cooperation.

3

NEW YORK CITY:
THE BIG APPLE

New York, New York. No other city in the world is like this one. No other city has the power to evoke so many different powerful images. Say "New York" to one person and he or she will think of the Empire State Building; someone else will immediately focus on the underground subway system. Others think of crime and fear and vice; still others recall the opera, ballet, and museums. Some picture the huge, green expanse of Central Park; others remember seeing the stark images of the decaying South Bronx filmed for national television.

GEOGRAPHY

New York City is largely made up of islands and parts of an island, surrounded by great rivers and the Atlantic Ocean. Separated into five sections called boroughs, New York City is, in a way, not just one but many different cities. Manhattan, the Bronx, Queens, Brooklyn, and Staten Island each have separate identities and individual atmospheres.

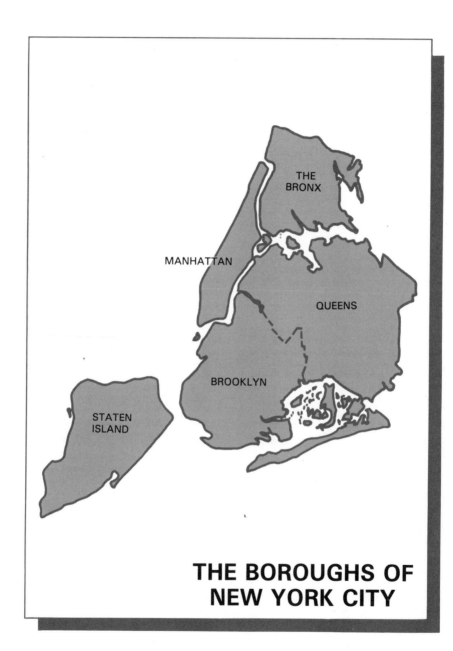

THE
BRONX

MANHATTAN

QUEENS

BROOKLYN

STATEN
ISLAND

THE BOROUGHS OF
NEW YORK CITY

Three rivers flow between and around the five boroughs. The Hudson River flows south 510 miles (820 km) from a tiny lake called Tear-in-the-Clouds, atop Mount Marcy in the Adirondack Mountains. The Hudson separates the island of Manhattan from the eastern shore of New Jersey.

The East River separates the western end of Long Island (which includes the boroughs of Brooklyn and Queens) from Manhattan and the only borough on the mainland, the Bronx. The East River is not technically a river at all, but a saltwater estuary, connecting New York Bay to the Long Island Sound, a distance of about 16 miles (26 km).

An 8-mile (13-km) waterway slanting around the northern end of Manhattan and separating the borough from the mainland is called the Harlem River.

BRIDGES & TUNNELS

At night New York's lighted bridges twinkle and glimmer as they connect parts of the city with one another. Perhaps the most inspiring of the bridges, the Brooklyn Bridge, celebrated its hundredth birthday in 1983. It was the first bridge to connect Manhattan and Brooklyn and has long inspired the imaginations of those who have seen it. It was the first suspension bridge to use steel-wire cables, and when it was completed in 1883, it was the longest bridge in the world.

Sixty-one other bridges have been built since then in the city, and four tunnels have been dug beneath the waterways. These tunnels, themselves marvels of technology, offer a means of crossing the waterways to people who drive in and out of the five boroughs.

THE SUBWAY

The traffic jams, honking horns, and taxicabs attest to the fact that many New Yorkers prefer to travel in the relative safety and convenience of automobiles. But every day over 5 million people travel on one of the largest transit systems in the world. Over 200 miles (320 km) of underground train routes stretch across the city.

The sights and sounds of a subway ride are unforgettable and incomparable. Beneath the sidewalks of New York, the subways have created almost a second city, with shops and newspaper and magazine stands. For a long time, crime has been rampant in these underground tunnels, yet the subways still provide the fastest, least expensive way to get around this huge city.

NEW YORK: THE MAGNET

Beautiful bridges and noisy subways are only two of the wonders of New York City. There are also hundreds of restaurants, art galleries, theaters, and banking institutions. There are approximately thirty-five four-year colleges and about 1,000 elementary and secondary schools. There are small, five-story apartment buildings, huge, ugly tenements, luxurious condominiums, and immense loft buildings.

But what is really special about the city is the people who live there. The people who were born and raised in New York and those who have come there from other places all share a special quality, a special resilience, a spirit that comes from being New Yorkers. The Russian Jew shares it with the Southern Baptist from Mississippi, the third-generation Italian shares it with the young college student from Iowa.

In the hundreds of neighborhoods throughout this city, the energy of 7 million New Yorkers makes itself felt. Not all of the energy is positive—there is crime, poverty, and despair. But there is also vitality and personality, and it is this that is the magnet of New York. The idea that absolutely anything is possible—the direst poverty, the most ostentatious wealth, the highest bridges, the scariest back alleys, the greatest musicals on any stage—is always there.

In the next few pages, you'll walk through some of New York

City's neighborhoods. You'll meet some of its citizens, see some of its fine architecture, feel some of its moods and atmosphere.

MANHATTAN

Manhattan, perhaps more than any other single place, has become an international symbol of progress, change, diversity, and excitement. It is considered by many to be the cultural and financial center of the world. Manhattan Island is 22 square miles (58 km) in area. Although only about 1.5 million people call Manhattan home, another 6 million go there to work. Every weekday, the sidewalks of Manhattan are jam-packed with people.

As in any city, New York has its share of crime, especially drug-related crime. There are huge pockets of poverty in one of the nation's wealthiest communities. Blacks, Hispanics, and other minorities still suffer the inequities of racial discrimination, and many white Americans join them in a seemingly endless cycle of poverty and despair.

What is most striking to Manhattan's visitors and residents, however, is not the crime or the drugs, but the marked increase in the number of homeless people living on the streets. These people sleep in doorways, eat out of garbage cans, and seem to have lost all hope of a better life. Some of them are just down on their luck, others are recently released psychiatric patients unable to manage on their own, and still others are addicted to drugs and/or alcohol.

Poverty, the homeless, crime, and drugs are all national problems—they exist in big cities and small towns across America. But because of the enormous concentration of wealth in Manhattan, these problems seem all the more severe in contrast.

Architects from all over the world have used Manhattan as a backdrop for their creations. The Empire State Building, the World Trade Center, and the United Nations building are just a few of the gems that make up the modern skyline that has become Manhattan's trademark. But it takes only a short walk between these glass-and-steel towers to discover another, older Manhattan. Historic landmarks abound in this city, including some of the country's oldest churches, synagogues, private homes, and theaters.

But more than its economic diversity, cultural wealth, and architectural history, it is the neighborhoods of Manhattan that give the city its true character. To really understand Manhattan, you must wander through its streets.

Lower Manhattan

Dominated by the 110-story twin towers of the World Trade Center, Lower Manhattan is the center of New York City's financial district. Wall Street is home to the New York Stock Exchange, which is the largest marketplace of securities in the world. International corporations and banks have offices there.

Looking down from the observation deck of the Trade Center, most eyes gaze first at New York Harbor. There the Statue of Liberty stands proudly, welcoming newcomers with her torch held high. Ellis Island, where millions of immigrants first landed on their way into the United States in the nineteenth and early twentieth centuries, is also in New York Harbor.

Lower Manhattan is the oldest part of the city, and the British had their stronghold there during the Revolutionary War.

Tribeca and Soho

Just a decade ago, these two neighborhoods were among the least developed in the city, having suffered an economic and population

A view of the New York Stock Exchange Building (right)—the hub of financial activity for the nation.

decline during the 1960s. Once the center for much of Manhattan's manufacturing industry, this area was filled with loft buildings, which emptied out as more and more industries left the city. Today many of these buildings have been converted into residential spaces, making this downtown area, just north of the financial district, a very popular neighborhood.

Some of the oldest buildings in the city have been renovated and preserved there. The latest paintings, sculptures, and photographs from newly recognized artists are on display in the art galleries that have made these neighborhoods so famous.

Little Italy and Chinatown

Two of the oldest ethnic areas in the city are just north and to the east of Soho. Little Italy has long been the mecca for Italian immigrants, and today second- and third-generation Italian-Americans make their home there, alongside new Italian immigrants and New Yorkers from every walk of life.

Chinatown is another world altogether, with its Chinese movie theaters and shops selling products from Taiwan, Hong Kong, and mainland China. It's hard to catch more than a few words of English on these city streets, since not only Chinese, but other Asians— from Vietnam, Thailand, Laos, and elsewhere—have flocked to Chinatown in recent years.

Greenwich Village and the Lower East Side

Greenwich Village is known for its long history of nonconformity and creativity. This small area in the western part of Lower Man-

Mott Street, the main thorough-fare in Chinatown, retains an authentic ethnic flavor.

hattan has long attracted freewheeling thinkers, political activists, and writers.

Some of its atmosphere certainly comes from the students who attend New York University, one of the largest schools in the country. Its campus is situated mainly around Washington Square Park, in the heart of the Village, but also extends throughout this most interesting and energetic community.

The Lower East Side was the home of millions of newly arrived immigrants in the eighteenth, nineteenth, and early twentieth centuries. First the Italians, then the Irish, the Poles, and the Russian Jews lived among astonishing filth in tiny one-room apartments, sometimes ten people to a room.

Today the Lower East Side and the East Village —a burgeoning neighborhood to the east of Greenwich Village and to the north of the Lower East Side —have found new life. Poles and Russians live alongside artists and students. Even the punk and New Wave rockers, with their shocking pink hair and black leather clothes, fit into this eclectic and erratic neighborhood.

Midtown

The steel, glass, and granite canyon that is midtown Manhattan is an explosive, hectic, expensive neighborhood. The headquarters of television studios, publishing companies, gold and silver dealers, theaters, museums, and some of the best shopping in the world attract millions of tourists and New Yorkers.

Midtown's centerpiece is the Empire State Building, which was the tallest building in the world when it was constructed in 1931,

Washington Square Park, in the heart of Greenwich Village. The marble arch was designed by architect Stanford White.

and is still the most recognizable building on Manhattan's skyline.

Rockefeller Center, which encompasses Forty-seventh to Fifty-second streets between Fifth and Sixth avenues, is almost a city within a city. Nearly 250,000 people work in Rockefeller Center's nineteen buildings every day—more than the population of all but sixty American cities! Radio City Music Hall, the nation's largest indoor theater, has its home in the RCA Building in the center. McGraw-Hill and Simon & Schuster, two major American publishers, also have their offices there. A public plaza, where people can ice-skate in the winter, sits in the middle of this extravaganza.

St. Patrick's Cathedral, the largest Roman Catholic church in the United States, is right across Fifth Avenue from Rockefeller Center. Broadway is in midtown too, along with numerous museums.

Central Park

In 1857, New York City sponsored a design competition for a public park. City dwellers desperately needed a little nature in their lives, as the urban landscape took more and more trees and grass away for roads and buildings. Two well-respected landscape architects, Calvert Vaux and Frederick Law Olmstead, won that competition and Central Park became a reality. An extraordinary 840 acres (340 hectares) of rolling hills and green grass were set right in the middle of the largest city in the world! The park stretches north from Fifty-ninth Street to 110th Street and from Fifth Avenue west to Central Park West.

Two and a half miles (4 km) long and a half mile (0.8 km) wide, the park is a lot of country in the big city. Central Park contains a zoo, playgrounds, a merry-go-round, and stables and horseback riding trails. The plays of Shakespeare and other dramatists are performed for free at the park's Delacorte Theatre every summer. There's also an ice-skating rink and a huge lake.

But more than these facilities, it is the open space that is so special about Central Park. Even at its most crowded, there are still

The Big Apple's skyline is magical at night.

Set amid the buildings of Manhattan,
Central Park is larger than the country of Monaco.

pockets of privacy and serenity to be found amid the formal gardens, groves of apple trees, and many fountains of Central Park.

Upper West Side

The Upper West Side is an ethnically and economically mixed neighborhood now experiencing a building and development boom. The neighborhood boasts all the ingredients that make New York itself a great city—unequaled cultural institutions, a great university, fine architecture, and a diverse population.

The Upper West Side is the site of Lincoln Center and Carnegie Hall, two of the most famous performing-arts centers in the world. Carnegie Hall was built in 1891 and has been the center for American classical music since it opened. Its magnificent acoustics have never been equaled anywhere, and its superb reputation attracts the best musicians from all over the world.

Lincoln Center is a complex of theaters, dance studios, and the country's foremost school of music, the Juilliard School. The Metropolitan Opera Company makes its home in the spectacular opera house there, and the New York City Ballet and New York City Opera both perform in theaters at Lincoln Center.

Columbia University, founded in 1754, is located between 116th and 121st streets. An intellectual mecca, Columbia has many illustrious faculty members and graduates, including Dwight D. Eisenhower who was president of the University from 1948 to 1951.

Just north and east of Columbia University lies Harlem, one of the largest black communities in the country. Almost half of New York City's 2 million blacks live there today, some in utter poverty and others working hard to create a solid core of middle-class prosperity.

Harlem's history is a rich and fascinating one. For a time in the late 1800s, it was considered one of the finest neighborhoods in New York. When blacks flocked to the North after World War I, they chose to settle in Harlem, where the rents were lower than in the center of New York. The 1920s were a time of great prosperity, in Harlem as well as in the rest of the country. The mellow and compelling strains of jazz could be heard in Harlem's famous nightclubs.

It wasn't until after World War II that the housing shortage and lack of jobs for blacks began to hit Harlem hard. Since then, its slums, high crime rate, and drug addiction problems have overshadowed its striving middle class. Even today, its population continues to decline and businesses to close.

The Upper East Side
On the other side of town, some of the world's wealthiest people reside on the tree-lined streets and wide avenues of Manhattan's Upper East Side. Although it has its share of ethnic enclaves and economic diversity, the Upper East Side is best known for its high concentration of the wealthy and powerful.

In addition to the luxury apartment buildings and private town houses that dominate this neighborhood, there are many fine cultural institutions and museums.

There are other neighborhoods in Manhattan, further uptown, further east, and further west. In fact, every block can seem like a different neighborhood, each with its own flavor.

The tour of New York City is far from over. The other four boroughs have enough history and population for each to be a city by itself. An overview of New York City would hardly be complete without a visit to each of them.

STATEN ISLAND

To most New Yorkers, Staten Island is only an aging pier where the famous ferry docks after its trip from the southern tip of Manhattan. But the island has a unique history. For many years, Staten Island was an agricultural region, and in fact it remains to this day the most rural of the five boroughs. In the 1830s, it was a quiet settlement of fishing and farming villages. Then its beaches became attractive to wealthy New Yorkers, who built mansions on the island.

The twentieth century brought a share of industry to Staten Island. Beer, soap, and chocolate were manufactured there. An industrial center was created along one of the island's main avenues, Victory Boulevard.

Staten Island is the least densely populated of the city's boroughs, with just about 250,000 residents on its 50 square miles (130 sq km). Although many people now live in large apartment buildings, most Staten Islanders live in private homes. Neighborhoods, many resembling small upstate towns, dot the borough.

The desperate need for affordable housing in New York City has pitted conservationists and civic groups against real estate developers. One project that delights both sides in this struggle is Staten Island's Snug Harbor Cultural Center. This 80-acre (32-hectares) haven for the arts was originally built in 1831 as a home for retired sailors. It is now undergoing a massive renovation and houses theaters, gallery spaces, and a soon-to-be completed music hall.

BROOKLYN

Brooklyn is the most populous borough of New York City. About 2.5 million people make their home within its 81 square miles (210 sq km). Since the 1600s, when the Dutch bought a small village from a tribe of Indians called the Canarsee, Brooklyn has been a vital part of the Big Apple.

The borough occupies the southeast extremity of Long Island and lies southeast of Manhattan across the East River. It is bounded on the east by Queens, on the west by New York Bay, and on the south by the Atlantic Ocean. It has over 200 miles (320 km) of waterfront, much of it beaches and parks.

Because of its size and long history, Brooklyn has developed almost as a separate city. In fact, it remained legally separate until

*This farmhouse is typical of the architecture
created by the settlers on Staten Island.*

The Brooklyn Bridge, linking Lower
Manhattan and downtown Brooklyn

1898. Today it would rank among the nation's major metropolises even if it weren't part of New York City. It has a bustling downtown full of factories, office buildings, and busy shopping districts. Its earlier economy focused on the enormous, but now discontinued, Brooklyn Navy Yard. It was there that many of the nation's warships were built and berthed.

As with Manhattan, it is the richness and vitality of Brooklyn's neighborhoods that is most remarkable. The choice residential section of Brooklyn Heights, with its fashionable brownstone buildings and magnificent view of Manhattan's skyline, is a haven for young professionals.

The neighborhood of Park Slope has Victorian rowhouses, once private homes for nineteenth-century Brooklyn families and now divided into apartments for modern city dwellers. A vital Orthodox Jewish community lives in the section of Brooklyn called Borough Park. One of the largest black communities in the world is found in Bedford-Stuyvesant. Some of the worst slums in America coexist in "Bed-Sty" with attractive brownstones and a growing middle class. A sign of urban decay and neglect is Brownsville, with its many blocks of low-income housing projects and burned-out or abandoned buildings.

One of Brooklyn's most famous areas is Coney Island—not an island at all, but a peninsula. New Yorkers have been escaping to Coney Island, once a festive vacation center but now in a decline, since the summers of the 1840s. Hotels, bright beach houses, a racetrack, and amusement parks were crowded onto this small strip of land. Today most of the beach houses have been torn down, low-income housing put up, and the parks have become shabby.

Brighton Beach was for many years an enclave for elderly Jews. Then, in the mid-1970s, a new wave of Russian Jews arrived in the area, earning it the nickname "Little Odessa," after a major Russian city. Just north of Brighton is Sheepshead Bay, where fishing boats are docked. Fish can be purchased right off the boats.

Although Manhattan, with all of its cultural opportunities, lies

Coney Island, once a popular summertime destination, has declined in recent years.

Shea Stadium accommodates over 55,000 fans.

just across the river, Brooklyn has impressive institutions of its own, including the Brooklyn Academy of Music and the Brooklyn Museum.

QUEENS

Another huge borough that could easily stand on its own as a separate city is Queens. Covering 118 square miles (306 sq km) on the southwest tip of Long Island, Queens is the home of nearly 2 million New Yorkers. Queens became part of New York City in 1898, having expanded rather slowly after the first Dutch settlers arrived in 1643. It wasn't until the subway went through the borough in the 1930s that it was fully developed by countless commuters wanting suburban homes. In 1936, the Mayor's Committee on City Planning estimated that the population of Queens would eventually be 1.9 million—an amazingly accurate prediction.

There are many quiet residential communities in this borough, places such as Forest Hills, Flushing, and Astoria. Long Island City is an aging industrial section of Queens now undergoing a rejuvenation.

Astoria, which borders on Long Island City, is itself undergoing a renewal of one of its earlier industries—moviemaking. In the 1920s, the motion picture business boomed in Queens, with stars such as the Marx Brothers and Gloria Swanson working out of what was then known as Lasky Studios. Today the flourishing Kaufman Astoria Studios occupy the same site and surrounding blocks. Films are being made out of the studios once again, as well as commercials for television.

It is the public spaces that are truly unusual in Queens. Flushing Meadows Park was the glamorous site of the 1939 and 1964-65 World's Fairs. The park includes Shea Stadium, the home of the "Amazing" Mets baseball team, winner of the 1986 National League pennant and World Series. The USTA National Tennis Center, where the U.S. Open Tournament is played every year, is also part of Flushing Meadows Park.

—51

The most generous stretches of land in Queens belong to the John F. Kennedy and La Guardia airports. National and international flights arrive and depart from these airports by the hundreds every day.

Wildlife refuges at both Jamaica Bay and the Alley Pond Environmental Center offer wildlife tours and a look at more than 300 species of birds and mammals. It is hard to imagine that so much undeveloped land exists in New York City, but nearly a quarter of this borough alone is preserved land.

THE BRONX

In 1641, a Scandinavian named Jonas Bronk bought 500 acres (202 hectares) of the New World from the Indians. The land Mr. Bronk purchased was pure, virgin forest. Today the Bronx is almost 42 square miles (109 sq km) of land on the mainland, contiguous with the lower part of the Hudson Valley. Most of it bears no resemblance to the wilderness that surrounded its founding father. The Hudson River flows past its western shore, and Long Island Sound ends off the eastern shore. Across the narrow of water formed by the joining of the East and Harlem rivers is Manhattan.

In the northern section of the Bronx, many neighborhoods retain their ethnic characters. One example is the "Little Italy" of the Bronx, called Belmont. The Enrico Fermi Center there is the nation's first Italian-American library.

The Bronx has seven fine college campuses, including Fordham University, Lehman College, and the Albert Einstein College of Medicine. Above University Heights (home of Fordham), tree-lined streets and suburban homes and lawns speak of middle-class stability.

Elephant riding is fun, especially at Wild Asia at the famous Bronx Zoo.

The center of the borough is an amazing stretch of wildlife and wilderness, bringing the early days of the Bronx to mind. The Bronx Botanical Gardens have some of the most exotic plants and flowers found in the country, and it sits amid a hemlock forest in the Bronx Park. The world-renowned Bronx Zoo is there too.

Unfortunately, it is the South Bronx that has attracted the most attention in America and around the world. During the late 1970s and 1980s, the South Bronx became synonymous with urban decay and blight. A seemingly endless cycle of neglect and abandonment began to take place in the 1960s as many businesses and the once strong middle class left the area. Slums spread, crime increased, more residents left the area. Landlords abandoned or burned down their buildings. Drug addicts, pushers, arsonists, and frightened elderly people and poor minorities were the only inhabitants.

When President Jimmy Carter visited the area during his 1976 election campaign, the Bronx became a symbol of everything that could go wrong with northern American cities, and plans were put into the works to rejuvenate the area. "Sweat equity" programs were attempted, whereby residents would be given ownership of buildings they themselves repaired and renovated. In this way, individuals would learn new skills at the same time they were fixing up a new place to live. The South Bronx Development Corporation is another agency determined to bring in new businesses, strengthen the ones that remain, and help smaller neighborhood groups renew their streets and apartment buildings.

Although it is far too soon to tell if these plans can work, one landmark of the South Bronx is the focus of millions of Americans' dreams every spring: Yankee Stadium, home to the New York Yankees baseball team.

THE UPSTATE
ADVENTURE

Now that you've seen the greatest city in the world, and walked through the densest population in America, you'll probably need to breathe some fresh, clean air. Millions of New York City dwellers escape the urban frenzy to find peace in any of a number of upstate regions just hours away from the city. From Long Island to the Adirondacks to the Finger Lakes and the Niagara Frontier, the upstate adventure is an experience you'll never forget.

LONG ISLAND

Technically part of New York City's metropolitan area (Brooklyn and Queens are two counties in western Long Island), Long Island is a strip of land 118 miles (190 km) long and 23 miles (37 km) wide at its widest point. Jutting out proudly from New York City into Long Island Sound, it is the largest island on the nation's Eastern Seaboard. It is a gift from the Ice Age. When the glaciers melted 10,000 years ago, they left behind a sand- and boulder-strewn island girdled by hundreds of miles of spectacular beaches, bluffs, wetlands, and natural harbors.

—55

Two and a half million people now make their home on the island. The western tip borders on New York City, and many Long Islanders make the commute to the city to work every day. Other residents find employment in any number of companies on the island itself. High-technology industries, including telecommunications, computers, and defense, have companies with headquarters or branches there. These successful enterprises, coupled with New York City's nearby resources, have brought Long Island a very low unemployment rate and a relatively high standard of living.

While high-tech dominates Long Island's economy, the area maintains its rich tradition in agriculture and fishing. Productive dairy and vegetable farms dot the island, and duck farming still thrives.

Tuna fishing has recently enjoyed a boom. On the northern tip, at Montauk, tuna fishermen have been making huge profits in an industry that drew $3,500 per year as recently as 1975. In 1985, however, tuna, sold mainly to Japanese importers, commanded as much as $7 per pound (0.45 kg), netting a whopping $1.8 million! The tuna business is yet another addition to Long Island's long history of living off the sea.

Whaling Ships and Pirates
Whales, those huge and mysterious sea mammals, were the quarry of American sailors for nearly 200 years. Brought to Long Island from New England, the whaling business was at its peak in the mid-1800s. Large migrations of whales passed by Long Island's coast, making whaling a highly adventurous, and profitable, local business. Whalers followed their quarry to all the world's oceans on voyages lasting up to five years. The whale oil these brave men brought back illuminated homes, fed industrial machinery, and was the ingredient of hundreds of products. The adventures the whalers had were written about by New York writers James Fenimore Cooper and Herman Melville.

Ghosts of pirate ships that once sailed off the island's coast are said to still haunt the waters on dark nights! The scoundrel Captain

A Long Island duck farm

Kidd is thought by some to have buried his treasure somewhere on Long Island.

THE HUDSON VALLEY
AND THE CATSKILLS

Less than an hour away from the hustle and bustle of New York City lies a splendid valley that is rich with historical significance and rural beauty, yet remains a center for high technology. The Hudson Valley has the fastest-growing population in New York State, but has maintained its reputation for delicious apples, productive dairy farms, and an atmosphere made famous by one of its special nineteenth-century residents, the author Washington Irving.

Some of the state's wealthiest suburbs are located at the southern edge of the valley, just bordering New York City. Further up the Hudson are the cities of Poughkeepsie and Beacon, long centers of tool, textile, and steel manufacturing and now host to a burgeoning high-technology community. In fact, the Hudson Valley is one of the few areas in the state that has been able to keep its manufacturing industry strong. IBM (International Business Machines), famous for its electronic office equipment, computers, and defense work, has its headquarters in Poughkeepsie, employing some 24,000 people.

The city of Poughkeepsie is also home to Vassar College, founded in 1861 by Matthew Vassar, a Poughkeepsie beer brewer. One of the first women's colleges in the United States, it thrives today as a coed university with an excellent reputation for scholarship.

While its cities continue to grow, the Hudson Valley's rural areas also blossom. Apple orchards, poultry and dairy farms, and the nation's oldest vineyard serve the area with its delectable products. Before the midwestern states became the nation's breadbasket, the valley also grew wheat and vegetables in great quantities, helping to feed a hungry new America.

New York State is the second largest producer of apples in the country.

The United States Military Academy at
West Point is in the Hudson Valley.

In many other ways, too, the Hudson Valley served as an important center of early America. Its fields, meadows, and shores were the sites of major Revolutionary War battles, especially at Newburgh, Fishkill, and West Point. In fact, George Washington had his military headquarters at White Plains and Newburgh throughout the war. Later, in 1809, the U.S. Military Academy was founded at West Point. It continues to train the nation's finest army officers.

Two presidents, Martin Van Buren and Franklin Delano Roosevelt, made their homes in the valley at one time. Both estates are now historical monuments, as are other great mansions built by wealthy industrialists in the 1800s and 1900s.

The Catskills

It is hard to believe that just a few hours drive from New York City lies 3,000 square miles (7,800 sq km) of mountains—some with peaks as high as 4,000 feet (1,200 m).

For a short time in the early 1800s, the Catskills thrived as a bustling commercial center. Turnpikes passed through the mountain-range community, connecting the southern and western parts of the state to Albany. Large mills were built to grind wheat, grown in the Hudson Valley and the Finger Lakes region, into flour to ship to New York City. Fur-trapping and leather-tanning were important industries as well.

But when the Erie Canal was built, making land transportation unprofitable, the Catskills began to rely on their most bountiful resource: the great outdoors. Millions of nearby city folk would pay good money to "get away from it all."

In fact, during Prohibition in the 1920s (when making, selling, and drinking alcoholic beverages was illegal), the Catskills were famous for illegal mountain-brewed applejack and moonshine whisky.

Today white-river rafting, rock-climbing, skiing, skating, hiking, and especially trout fishing are just a few of the things you can do in the Catskills. Although the Catskills have recently suffered serious economic times, tiny villages and small towns are still populated by innkeepers, craftspeople, and winegrowers.

CENTRAL NEW YORK

A little more than ten years ago, the United States had its two-hundredth birthday. In 1986, Albany, New York, celebrated its *Tri-centennial*—300 years as a chartered city, one of the oldest in the country. First known as Fort Nassau, then Bervrwyk, Fort Orange, and finally Albany, this city was first settled as a Dutch fur-trading post long before the Pilgrims landed at Plymouth, Massachusetts, in 1620.

The capital of New York is now a modern city, a cultured center of government, education, and the arts. Since 1797, Albany has served as the seat of government for New York, and its grand Capitol Building boasts of the pride New Yorkers have for their state and its leaders.

Known for its architecture, this building covers nearly 3½ acres (1.4 hectares, or 14,100 sq m), almost as many as the U.S. Capitol in Washington, D.C. Inside it is full of finely crafted stone and wood carvings that line the hallways and adorn the Executive Chamber, Senate, and Assembly Halls. The building's interior stone architecture and supporting arches awed construction experts of the day (1867-1897). One of its most delightful features is its "Million Dollar" staircase, which rises 119 feet (36 m) from the first to the fourth floor in a breathtakingly graceful curve.

The Capitol Building is just one of the many architectural delights in Albany. Theater and dance thrive at the Empire State Institution for the Performing Arts, called the "Egg" because of its unique oval shape. The Egg is part of a larger project, the Empire State Plaza, planned and built during Governor Nelson Rockefeller's administration. Eleven modern glass-and-marble structures provide a fascinating contrast to the old Victorian and Georgian houses that make up most of the city.

*The Capitol Building in Albany is known
for its impressive architecture.*

Culturally, Albany ranks among the top smaller cities in the country, with five world-renowned museums and a fine symphony orchestra that attracts New Yorkers from all over the state. Its Dutch heritage is alive as well, with its annual Tulip Festival and Pinkersfest; tulips blossom throughout the city, and children, dressed in Dutch costumes, scrub the city's main street until it sparkles.

Albany also has a unique "inland" seaport—one of the busiest ports in the Northeast. Oceangoing ships sail up the Hudson, bringing everything from foreign cars to bananas. Grain from the Midwest is brought here to be processed and shipped to other regions, and an oil refinery does the same to oil. This industrious, modern side of Albany is delightfully set off by its reverence for history and its graceful architecture.

Throughout this entire region, in fact, an impressive balance has been struck between city and country and the new and the old. To the north, Saratoga Springs remains a fashionable resort, especially in August, when its world-famous thoroughbred racetrack is in full-swing. All year round, tourists come to enjoy the quiet, small-town friendliness and perhaps take a "cure" at the Roosevelt Spa. The spa was the original drawing card to the town back in the nineteenth century, when a mineral spring was discovered there. These waters were thought to have medicinal value for all kinds of ailments. Although modern science has discredited these claims, people still come to enjoy the calming, soothing effects of the famous spring water. Saratoga's Performing Arts Center, the summer home of the New York City Ballet and Philadelphia Orchestra, has an impressive reputation, attracting tourists and residents alike.

A car being unloaded at the port of Albany—one of the busiest ports in the Northeast.

The world-famous Saratoga Racetrack, where races are held only during the month of August

To the north and east of Saratoga is a countryside made famous by one of America's most beloved painters, the late Grandma Moses. Among the lush hills and meadows, productive dairy and vegetable farms show both the peacefulness of the region and the hardworking nature of its population. They also provide a rather striking contrast to the mill towns and industrial cities that lie to the southwest, along the Mohawk and Susquehanna rivers.

Each of the cities in this region has its own unique history and charm. Troy, for instance, was one of the first cities settled in New York, and in the 1820s and 1830s it became the center for three nationwide scientific and educational movements.

Amos Easton spurred public interest in mechanical and scientific development when he was appointed senior professor at the Rensselaer Polytechnic Institute, a world-renowned school specializing in the sciences that continues to educate today.

The Emma Willard School for Girls, still one of the finest preparatory schools for girls in the region, was founded by liberal-education pioneer Emma Willard in Troy in 1821. A year later, scientist Henry Burden came to Troy with his inventions that dramatically stimulated the city's iron industry.

Schenectady, lying along the Mohawk River, retained much of its Dutch and English background while evolving into a modern city. The very first railroad in New York State, called the "DeWitt Clinton," ran from Albany to Schenectady in 1831. In 1848, the first locomotive factory was organized there, and it became the largest factory of its kind in the country. Schenectady became the railroad capital of the nation.

Thomas Alva Edison, one of the world's most important inventors, bought two factory buildings in Schenectady to found the General Electric Company in 1886. General Electric, now a multinational corporation, still makes its headquarters there.

The entire region, which also includes the cities of Cohoes, Rensselaer, Utica, Rome, and Binghamton, has a compelling history and hundreds of things to see and enjoy.

The Mohawk River in central New York

This area has long been the center of the state's manufacturing, electric, and transportation equipment, and paper industries. It is home to General Electric, Revere Copper and Brass, Special Metals, Inc., Endicott-Johnson Shoes, and other related companies. For a long time the region was a bustling, growing industrial community, but in the last few decades it has suffered, as has much of the Northeast, from a decline in population and a general shift away from manufacturing to service-related employment—real estate, banking, and financial services.

Fortunately, the public-service economy centered around the state capital has eased this decline. Government workers in Albany and the air force personnel at Griffis Air Force Base in Rome employ over one-quarter of the region's population. Besides keeping the state running smoothly, these employees also create a large market for the finance, insurance, and real estate fields. This allows an important shift from manufacturing to service-related jobs to take place.

The rich farmland, and the extensive railroad and waterway transportation systems, have kept agriculture strong, too. Poultry, dairy, and vegetable farms supply cities near and far with their products.

Tourism is big business here as well, with much for the public to see and experience. From Binghamton to Albany to Saratoga, the geological, cultural, and architectural wonders abound.

THE NORTH COUNTRY

Nowhere in the state is the concept of the "great outdoors" of a starker reality than here in the North Country. From the Adirondack Mountains to the nation's "Fourth Coastline" at the Thousand Islands and the St. Lawrence Seaway, the North Country is a spectacle of beauty. It is a panorama of mountain peaks, dense forests, sparkling lakes, and tiny islands.

Camping is a favorite activity in the Adirondacks.

The Adirondacks

Mount Marcy, sometimes known as "the Cloud Spitter," is 5,344 feet (1,629 m) high—the highest peak in the Adirondack Mountains. Below its summit is a small lake, appropriately called Lake Tear-in-the-Clouds, and it is here that the Hudson River has its beginning. Mount Marcy is the centerpiece of one of the most beautiful mountain ranges in the country.

Six million acres, 9,000 square miles (23,300 sq km)—an area roughly the size of the entire state of Vermont—the Adirondacks Park is the country's largest wilderness area outside of Alaska. The Adirondacks are a mountain range made up of rocks more than a billion years old. Its peaks and valleys were created by the glaciers of three ice ages, and its 2,000 lakes were left behind when the ice retreated 10,000 years ago. Pine, hemlock, and northern hardwood trees densely fill its acres. Beaver, raccoon, bear, deer, and even the endangered bald eagle make their homes in this spectacular, protected woodland.

The first human inhabitants were probably Algonkian Indians. They arrived in the area perhaps as long as 1,800 years before the first white people settled there in the early 1600s. The name Adirondack itself is thought to have come from a Mohawk Indian word meaning "tree-eater," which is what the Mohawks called the Algonkians who hunted and trapped in these mountains. The Indians believed that the highest mountain peaks, forty-six of which are over 4,000 feet high (1,200 m), were "sacred and mysterious" places and left them unexplored.

Although the white people's reverence for the mountains was not quite so religious, a profound respect for the area's extraordinary ecological and geographic qualities developed quite early. The mountainous terrain made large-scale farming impractical and rapid transportation almost impossible. The cruel winters, with temperatures that hover around the 0° F (−18° C) mark and storms that blanket the area under 20 feet (6 m) of snow, discouraged many people from attempting to settle there.

Until the mid-1800s, the Adirondacks were largely untouched by all but the hardiest explorers. Then, in 1849, a young man named Joel T. Headly published a book called *The Adirondacks or Life in the Woods.* In it, he described the clean, crisp mountain air and the good effect it had on his health. As the cities grew more crowded, and the railroads made traveling easier, curiosity about the North Country was being satisfied by more and more New Yorkers.

During the mid-1800s and into the 1900s, New York was the country's leading producer of lumber, and it was here in the Adirondacks that much of our nation's building products were produced. Pulpwood from this area is still a major source for paper and paper products, especially for the publishing industry centered in New York City. Unfortunately, the paper manufacturing process produces toxic (poisonous) air pollution. Known as acid rain, it falls into lakes and oceans when it rains.

Without some very perceptive planning, in fact, the entire region might have been lost to greedy land speculators, developers, and business people. But, by the turn of the century, the state government moved to protect the entire area from overdevelopment and depletion of natural resources. Forty percent of the area was declared "forever wild," with the remaining 60 percent privately owned, but strictly zoned. The public and private lands are not separated, but instead form an intriguing patchwork of 132 campsites, hundreds of antique and craft shops, and private estates, ski resorts, and animal preserves.

All year round, the outdoor adventure is enjoyed by some 9 million visitors. Lake Placid, host to the 1932 and 1980 Winter Olympics, is now a year-round Olympic Training Center, as well as a family-oriented ski town. The Adirondack Museum at Blue Mountain Lake is a huge, 30-acre (12-hectare or 121,500-sq-m) museum filled with displays of Adirondack history, art, and culture. And, although there are plenty of other museums, historical sites, and cultural centers to visit, it is the outdoors that people most enjoy about the area.

*Lake Placid, with Whiteface Mountain
in the background*

The Eisenhower Locks in the Thousand Islands region

The Nation's
"Fourth Coastline"

Descending from the western slopes of the Adirondacks, dropping from 2,600-foot-high (790 m) peaks down through 60 miles (97 km) of rolling hill country to wide lake and river plains, this region of New York is a true frontier. It is here that the green of upstate New York meets the blue of Lake Ontario and the St. Lawrence River. It is here that the dense forest gives way to dairy farms and apple orchards. Known as "America's Fourth Coastline," this region is composed of 150 miles (240 km) of farm-lined shores and waterways broken up by nearly 1,800 small islands.

An extension of the Erie Canal and Barge Canal systems, the St. Lawrence Seaway opened in 1959. A series of connecting locks, lakes, and rivers converts the 602-foot (183-m) rise from the mouth of the St. Lawrence River to the Great Lakes into a smooth trade route. The Seaway now carries ships bearing the products of American agriculture and industry from Chicago, Detroit, and Toledo to the Atlantic Ocean and world markets. The annual traffic is estimated at over 50,000 tons; over the years, some $200 billion worth of goods have been transported through this man-made wonder.

Further to the south, the Thousand Islands form a unique border between the United States and Canada:—"The jewels in the crown of the Empire State"—1,753 tiny islands crowd 50 miles (80 km) of the St. Lawrence where it opens into Lake Ontario. Some as small as 2 feet (0.6 m) square, others as large as 20 miles (32 km) square, these islands are known for their friendly people and their reverence for the sea that surrounds them.

The islands were discovered in the early seventeenth century by French explorer Jacques Cartier, who first named them. The French, British, and early Americans fought fierce and bitter battles in these waters, especially during the War of 1812. Today nearly two-thirds of the islands belong to Canada.

Agriculture and hydroelectric power form the region's healthy economy. Tourism, too, provides a great deal of income, as vacationers from all over the state flock to this unique community.

FINGER LAKES

Eleven long, sparkling lakes, set amid rolling green hills and pleasant farming villages, make up the centerpiece of this unique and vital region of New York. Dramatic gorges and waterfalls complete an unforgettable landscape.

It is a landscape made for dreaming, and throughout history, the Finger Lakes have inspired some of New York's finest thinkers and their innovative ideas. DeWitt Clinton was first inspired to build the Erie Canal as he watched the waterfalls in his hometown of Ithaca. Ezra Cornell decided to found his great university, Cornell, in Ithaca as well.

Joseph Smith lived for some time on a farm in the small town of Palmyra. It is here that he is said to have had the vision that led him to found the Mormon religion, which today has 3 million American members.

Samuel Langhorne Clemens, the American writer better known as Mark Twain, lived and worked in the town of Elmira. Strangely enough, it was in this northern New York town that he wrote *The Adventures of Huckleberry Finn* and *Tom Sawyer,* which are so rich in down-South Mississippi atmosphere.

Harriet Tubman, a runaway slave, made her home in Auburn, New York, after she escaped from slavery in Maryland. Aided by the strong abolitionist sentiments in this region of the state, she turned her home into a station on the Underground Railroad and led some 300 slaves to freedom in the North.

Susan B. Anthony and Elizabeth Cady Stanton both lived in the Finger Lakes area during their adult years, and it was here that the modern women's rights movement began. Seneca Falls was the site of the first women's rights convention, and the National Women's Hall of Fame opened there in 1979.

Today the Finger Lakes region is known not only because of its historical significance and physical beauty, but also for its excellent wines. The second largest wine-producing area in America

The Finger Lakes area is grape country.
Here wine is being aged in casks.

and the largest outside the state of California, the Finger Lakes boast two dozen wineries, producing from 1,500 to 20,000 cases of wine a year. New York wines receive serious attention and high praise from wine experts all over the world.

Although many of the smaller cities in the region have been extremely hard hit by the closing of industrial and manufacturing plants, the two main cities of Syracuse and Rochester remain busy centers. Both blossomed after the Erie Canal was built; but now that manufacturing has declined, each has faced its economic problems in a different way.

Syracuse lies at the very center of New York State and is its center for the manufacture of a diverse range of products—typewriters, electric and air-conditioning equipment, cast-stone building blocks, and traffic signals, to name just a few. But what Syracuse is probably best known for is salt. In fact, Syracuse is known as "Salt City."

Rich salt springs were discovered in what appeared to be a useless swamp by a French settler, Father Simon LeMoyne, in 1654. One of the most important salt settlements there was Salina, also called Salt Point, which is now the northern section of a bustling city. Syracuse's early economy was based on its ability to harvest and process salt, but it has now turned to finance and real estate to take up the slack.

Rochester, on the other hand, has become home to some of the most successful high-technology companies in the country, including Eastman-Kodak, Xerox, and Bausch & Lomb. Once known as Flour City because of the multitude of mills to process flour, Rochester has evolved into a thoroughly modern, high-tech community.

WESTERN NEW YORK

Western New York's greatest attraction is Niagara Falls. The sight of the 182-foot-high (55 m), 3,175-foot-wide (968 m) crashing wall

*Niagara Falls—western New York's
most popular attraction.*

of water is truly breathtaking. The hydroelectric power plant, a man-made wonder 5 miles (8 km) below the falls, is also awesome. Technology has made it possible to harness the many tons of water that pass over the falls every day and convert it to energy—enough energy to light the equivalent of 24 million 100-watt bulbs!

Every year ten million tourists travel to Western New York.

Buffalo, the state's second largest metropolitan area, was a small frontier outpost until 1825, when the completion of the Erie Canal turned it into one of the world's great inland ports.

Today Buffalo is suffering through rough economic times, as factories continue to close, leaving many Buffalo residents unem-ployed. Though often dismissed as simply a declining industrial center, Buffalo is a city with strong pride, thanks in large part to its thriving ethnic neighborhoods. Germans, Poles, Irish, Hungarians, and Italians have all lived and worked in Buffalo since the 1800s, and every year the city celebrates this diverse history with pa-rades and festivals. Buffalo has the biggest St. Patrick's Day Parade outside of New York City, and the biggest Pulaski Day parade, a celebration of Polish heritage, east of Chicago.

As with most of upstate New York, rich farmland and gentle rolling hills provide a delightful contrast to the bustling cities and waterways. Vineyards and fruit orchards stretch across the region, hardwood forests cover the hills, and lakes dot the valleys. Bordered by lakes and harbors famous for fishing and boating, this region includes New York's largest state park—the Allegheny. Seventy-five miles (120 km) of marked trails amid 65,000 primitive acres (26,300 hectares) are perfect for biking, camping, fishing, and hunting.

Nowhere in the state is the Indian heritage more pronounced than here at the southwest gateway to New York. Four Indian res-

*One of New York State's greatest
resources: the outdoors*

ervations—the Tuscarora and Tonawanda reservations, both near Buffalo, and the Cattaraugus and Allegheny reservations—are found in this area. Salamanca is the only American city located on an Indian reservation, the Allegheny, and it proudly displays Indian culture and history at two museums, the Seneca-Iroquois National Museum and the American Indian Crafts Center.

One of the oldest and greatest of this region's assets is the Chautauqua Institution, located on the western shore of the 22-mile-long (35 km) Chautauqua Lake. This learning and cultural center has attracted some of America's finest minds and most gifted performers since it was founded in 1874. Today its nine-week summer session offers a unique combination of arts, education, religion, and the great outdoors to thousands of students, teachers, and visitors.

CONCLUSION

As the state of New York enters the twenty-first century, it faces a number of challenges, some common to the rest of the nation and some unique to its own particular situation. It must continue to fight against the economic despair that plagues the Northeast as the steel industry and manufacturing continue to decline. The pollution of its air and water must be better monitored and controlled. And the multiple complexities of New York City provide its citizens, government officials, and visitors with both serious problems and a host of exciting opportunities for change and growth.

Since the earliest Indians enjoyed its lush splendor, New York has been a land of riches. From the bright lights of Broadway to the roar of Niagara Falls, New York State is a mosaic of big-city energy, small-town charm, and daring wilderness. The tour you have just taken through its main streets and back roads is only the beginning.

NEW YORK TODAY:
FACTS AT A GLANCE

Size: 47,831 square miles (123,822 sq km), plus 1,745 square miles (4,520 sq km) of inland water

Highest point: Mount Marcy, 5,344 feet (1,629 m)

Lowest point: sea level along Atlantic Ocean

Number of natural lakes: over 4,000

Greatest distance, east-west: 432 miles (695 km)

Greatest distance, north-south: 307 miles (494 km)

Atlantic coastline: 127 miles (204 km)

Shoreline: 775 miles (1,250 km)

Rivers and streams: 70,000 miles (112,650 km)

Major mountain ranges: Adirondack, Catskill, Shawangunk, and Taconic

Number of Adirondack Mountains over 4,000 feet (1,220 m): 46

Major inland lakes: Canandaigua, Cayuga, Champlain, Chautauqua, Conesus, Cranberry, Erie, George, Hemlock, Keuka, Loon, Oneida, Ontario, Otisco, Otsego, Owasco, Placid, Raquette, Sacandaga, Saranac, Schroon, Seneca, Skaneateles, Tupper

Major rivers: Allegheny, Ausable, Black, Chemung, Chenango, Delaware, East, Genesee, Hudson, Mohawk, Niagara, Oswego, Susquehanna, Unadilla

Major waterfalls: Ithaca (there are over 200 in the city and its environs); Niagara (182 feet, or 55 m); Portageville (110 feet, or 34 m); Taughannock (215 feet, or 66 m)

POPULATION/GOVERNMENT

People . . . it's New York's people that really make the difference! Of almost every race, color, and religion, New Yorkers live in crowded cities, tiny villages, and everything in-between.

Population: 17,557,288

Median age of residents: 32

Capital: Albany (population 101,727)

Type of government: Executive, bicameral legislature; meets annually. Governor elected by popular vote for four-year term. Senate—60 members; Assembly—150 members

Number of counties: 62

Number of cities: 62

Largest city: New York City (population 7,071,639)

Population density, New York State: 371 per square mile (2.59 sq km)

Population density, New York City: 23,494 per square mile (2.59 sq km)

Number of towns, villages: 931 towns; 557 incorporated villages

Population, urban: 84.6 percent

Population, rural: 15.4 percent

Portion of land area, rural or wild: 85 percent

TRANSPORTATION

Throughout New York's history, its transportation system has been one of its greatest assets, and it is as true today as it was back in pioneer times. Thanks to its waterways and airports, highways, railroads, and country roads, New York has remained a leader in industry, agriculture, and tourism.

Number of passenger vehicles registered: 7,774,000

State highway system mileage: 14,606 miles (23,505 km) plus 559-mile (900-km) New York State Thruway

Total state and local highway mileage: 109,485 miles (176,194 km)

Number of landing facilities: 471 (including 365 airports)

Number of scheduled airlines serving state: 48

Number of seaports handling 100,000 tons or more: 13

Largest air-cargo center: John F. Kennedy Airport (largest air-cargo center in the world)

Railroad track mileage: 4,000 miles (6,400 km), operated by twenty-eight railroads

EDUCATION

DeWitt Clinton was just one of the pioneers in American education, and he began in New York a tradition of excellent and varied education. Cornell University, an Ivy League school, is situated in Ithaca, while another Ivy League institution, Columbia University, educates thousands every year in New York City. In between, thousands of public and private schools, colleges, and universities in every field and for every price range exist. New York is also proud of its State University program which has sixty-four campuses.

Years of compulsory education: From ages 6 to 16

Number of public elementary and secondary schools: 4,074

Public elementary and secondary school enrollment: 2,748,397

Number of private elementary and secondary schools: 2,239

Private elementary and secondary school enrollment: 576,439

Number of higher education institutions and branches: 294 (most in U.S.)

Number of bachelor's degrees awarded: 85,133 (most in U.S.)

Number of master's degrees awarded: 32,845 (most in U.S.)

State university system: 64 campuses (4 university centers, 12 colleges of arts and sciences, Empire State nonresidential college [campus without walls], 4 medical centers, 6 agricultural and technical colleges, 4 specialized colleges, 5 statutory colleges, and 34 community colleges)

Largest 4-year college: New York University, enrollment 45,524

Smallest 4-year college: St. Anthony's-on-Hudson

AGRICULTURE

Over one-third of New York State is made up of farm acreage. Rich, fertile soil and a temperate climate make New York a leader in agriculture for the nation.

Total farm acreage: 919 million acres (4 million hectares)

Number of farms: 49,000

Average farm size: 202 acres (81.7 hectares, or 817,500 sq m)

Value of agricultural products: $2.6 billion

Amount of wine produced: 34 million gallons (second highest in U.S.)

Number of wineries: 52

FOR FURTHER READING

Adams, Arthur G. *The Hudson Through the Years.* Westwood, New Jersey: Lind Graphics Publications, 1983.

Carmer, Carl. *The Susquehanna.* New York: Rinehart & Co., 1955.

Wilson, Edmund. *Upstate: Records and Recollections of Northern New York.* New York: Farrar, Straus & Giroux, 1971.

INDEX

ABOUT THE AUTHOR

Suzanne LeVert is a free-lance writer and consultant in urban affairs in New York City. She has written two other books for young adults. She lives in Manhattan with her cat, Phoebe, and visits her beautiful seaside hometown of Rockport, Massachusetts, as often as possible.

DATE DUE

NOV 1 7 1989		
JAN. 2 2 1990		
1992		
FEB		
FEB. 1 3 1990		
APR. 1 1991		
	OCT 1 8 1990	

Demco, Inc. 38-293